EAA
OSHKOSH

**the world's biggest
aviation event**

Osprey Colour Series

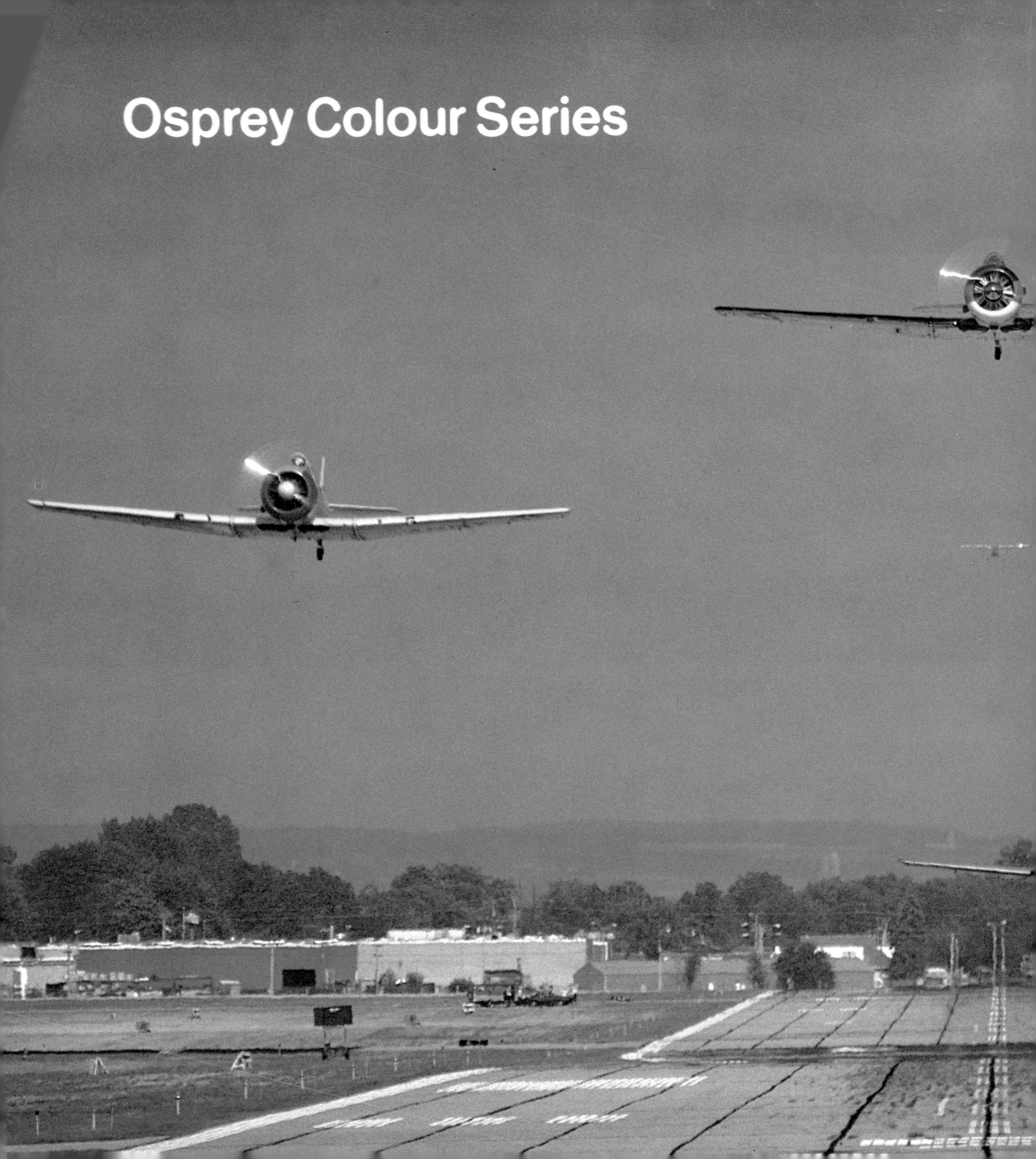

EAA OSHKOSH

the world's biggest aviation event

Nigel Moll

Published in 1985 by Osprey Publishing Limited
12–14 Long Acre, London WC2E 9LP
Member company of the George Philip Group

ISBN 0-85045-612-6

Editor Dennis Baldry
Designed by David Tarbutt
Printed in Hong Kong

In memory of Stephen Piercey and Cliff Barnett.

'Where are you going for your summer vacation?'

'To Oshkosh. We go there every year.'

'Oshkosh? Where in heck is Oshkosh?'

'It's in dairyland, Wisconsin, beside Lake Winnebago, a holy place where airplane people gather by the hundreds of thousands in late July for the biggest aviation event on Earth. I'm flying out there in my homebuilt airplane with our eldest son, and my wife is bringing the other kids in the camper.'

'Did you say *homebuilt* airplane?'

'Yes, built it myself in the garage from a kit. The factory-built ones were getting too expensive, and I think they're kinda dull anyway. Mine has everything I want from an airplane—two seats, room for some baggage, and it runs on the same stuff I put in the car. But it does 200 mph, and handles like a little fighter.'

'Is it legal . . . safe?'

'Yes, both, thanks in large part to the outfit that organizes the Oshkosh event—the Experimental Aircraft Association. Many years ago the EAA was formed to steer people like me— sport-flying enthusiasts—into a cohesive band that does its thing sensibly, legally and safely.'

'Are there many people like you who fly around just for fun in airplanes they built at home.'

'You bet. The EAA has nearly 100,000 members. Some of them not only build their own airplanes but design them as well.'

'What do these people do when they get to Oshkosh?'

'They eat, breathe and sleep airplanes and flying for a week. Some fly in, some drive, some hitch, some come from overseas. Some camp under their wings, some bring campers and tents, some stay in the University dorms and others move in as paying guests of Oshkosh households. The hotels fill up fast. During the day they listen in on forums that cover every conceivable interest in sport aviation; they watch a spectacular air show, browse through a flea market and static aircraft displays, row upon row; they get sore feet and a crick in the neck, and they love it. As dusk falls, the barbecue smoke and airplane stories begin to rise.'

Nigel Moll Cranbury, New Jersey

Nigel Moll is the Executive Editor of *FLYING*, the world's most widely read aviation magazine. He works out of New York City. His first book in this series, *RENO: Air Racing Unlimited*, also published by Osprey Publishing Limited and first printed in 1983, won the Aviation/Space Writers Association National Photography Award and the Earl D. Osborn Award for general aviation journalism that year. Moll has attended the EAA's Oshkosh convention for the past six years, but only at the most recent one did he get the full flavour by pitching tent in Camp Scholler with like-minded friends from England, California and Minnesota. The photographs in this book, like those in *RENO*, were taken with Nikon and Olympus 35 mm cameras and lenses, loaded with Kodachrome 25 and 64.

Contents

What is the EAA?

It stands for Experimental Aircraft Association, a term that the uninitiated might find somewhat alarming. Lay people are surprised to hear that not only are there ordinary folks out there building their own flying machines, but that they belong to a large, organized band of fellow enthusiasts. Furthermore, it's legal.

Since its establishment in 1953, however, the EAA has grown to appeal to every man, woman and child who loves flying for the sport of it. Its members fervently support the cause. The man behind the EAA's expression of that cause is Paul Poberezny (**left**), aided by his wife, Audrey, and son, Tom, and in more recent years by a loyal staff of full-time employees.

Paul Poberezny—official callsign Red One, and unofficially Pope Paul—inspires an almost religious fervor in his followers. As he drives his distinctive topless VW Beetle among the flock at Oshkosh, he draws from many the sense of awe one would associate with royalty. The spell is just as quickly lifted as he extends his hand, big smile spreading, and enquires, 'How's it going?' The common touch, to which the members respond with questions, suggestions, the occasional gripe. Paul will always lend an ear. He won't always agree, and he will say so. But he will remember, and the feedback from the flock will influence his

9

course. Paul has many facets: communicator, motivator, showman, administrator, experienced pilot, aircraft designer, organizer. Son Tom shares these attributes and, in his role of convention chairman, he needs them. The EAA is the Pobereznys, and whether or not their every move is endorsed, they have built up enormous respect from many sport pilots.

Although the EAA's roots are in the homebuilding movement, it also represents enthusiasts and owners of warbirds, antiques and classics, and ultralights, as well as amateur aerobatic pilots. There are nearly 700 chapters worldwide to promote activity at the local level. These chapters put out newsletters and hold meetings at which builders exchange tips; they also sponsor fly-ins.

EAA provides a voice in Washington for sport aviation to speak out about proposed legislation, of which there is plenty. Another valuable service is the nationwide designee program, under which some 900 experts work with members and their projects to help them meet high standards of airplane construction.

Oshkosh recently became the EAA's home, as well as the venue for its annual fly-in and convention, with the opening of the EAA Aviation Center and Air Museum. Operated by the EAA's Aviation Foundation, the museum contains some 80 aircraft and has been seen by more than 200,000 people since opening.

The EAA's role is as important as ever today: factory-built airplanes are still beyond the means of most private individuals; airspace is becoming more tightly controlled every year; fuel is pricey (although the EAA has cleared a path around this—autogas). But people still love to fly.

Previous page EAA Aviation Center and Air Museum. **Below** Paul Poberezny, founder and president of the EAA. **Right** Tom Poberezny, president of the EAA Aviation Foundation

Left Three Pitts Specials are fixed in a bomb-burst display in the Aviation Center's entrance tower. **Above** Grumman Duck on dry land inside the Air Museum

Above Until recently, the Stits Sky Baby was the smallest manned airplane ever to fly. It has a wing span of just seven feet, two inches, length of nine feet, 10 inches, and a cruise speed of 165 mph on 85 hp. It landed at 60 mph. **Below** Molt Taylor's 1950 Aerocar, the best of both worlds. **Right** Don Taylor's round-the-world Thorp T-18, still with long-range tank in the cabin

Homebuilts: dreams take wing

To fly an airplane that you built yourself, and maybe even designed yourself, is to take the thrill of flight a large step farther. It begins as a dream, but many thousands of persevering pilots have fulfilled that vision by transforming stacks of raw materials into real, full-size flying machines. Most of them are single-seaters or two-placers, and methods of construction vary widely.

For many years, homebuilts had the reputation of being fairly crude, if not in execution, at least in design for the sake of simplicity. Most were made of wood and fabric, all wood or a mixture of wood, fabric and steel tube. Few looked particularly racy or sassy, however imaginative the paint job; but in the 1970s there were some important developments.

First came the acceptance of composites as a material for making airplanes; second came the rediscovery of the canard configuration, in which the aerodynamic stabilizing surface is moved from the tail to the nose. It's a layout as old as powered flying: the Wright Brothers' Flyer of 1903 was stabilized thus, but despite the appearance of 'tail-first' designs throughout the history of aviation, it was the engine-in-the-front-and-tail-in-the-back layout that presided. Burt Rutan was the person who resurrected the canard and fired the imaginations of the homebuilders; they have built his designs (the Vari-Viggen, Quickie, VariEze and LongEze) by the thousands. Each year at Oshkosh, there are more 'Rutans' than any other single brand. Rutan's fertile mind has done a lot to modernize the technology of homebuilding. While a few designers

have followed his use of the canard, many have adopted composites. Composites can be less pleasant to work with than the old techniques, but they give the designer great flexibility. Where compound curves used to be avoided as too time consuming, they are now as easy to embody as simple curves. And to the builder's benefit, his creation begins to look like an airplane at quite an early stage; the self motivation thus comes more easily than it would have with a pile of ribs, stringers and spars that had consumed hundreds of hours and still looked nothing more than an elaborate exercise in woodworking.

Some of the more complex high-performance homebuilts are highly labour intensive, with perfectionist builders spending perhaps 5000 hours on their construction over 10 years. Some homebuilts are made from plans, while others come in kits. As long as the builder is responsible for at least 51 percent of the work required to make the airplane, it can be certificated in the Experimental category as an amateur-built aircraft intended for recreational purposes. Homebuilts cannot be flown for hire, used commercially, rented or leased.

In line with the aim of keeping down the cost of flying, the EAA has recently embarked on a program of flight-testing to gain approval for the use of autogas in many airplanes, factory-built ones included. Avgas is expensive (about $2.00 a gallon) and scarce in some parts of the world.

Page 16 Rutan Voyager. **Preceding page and these pages** Flocks of VariEzes grazing

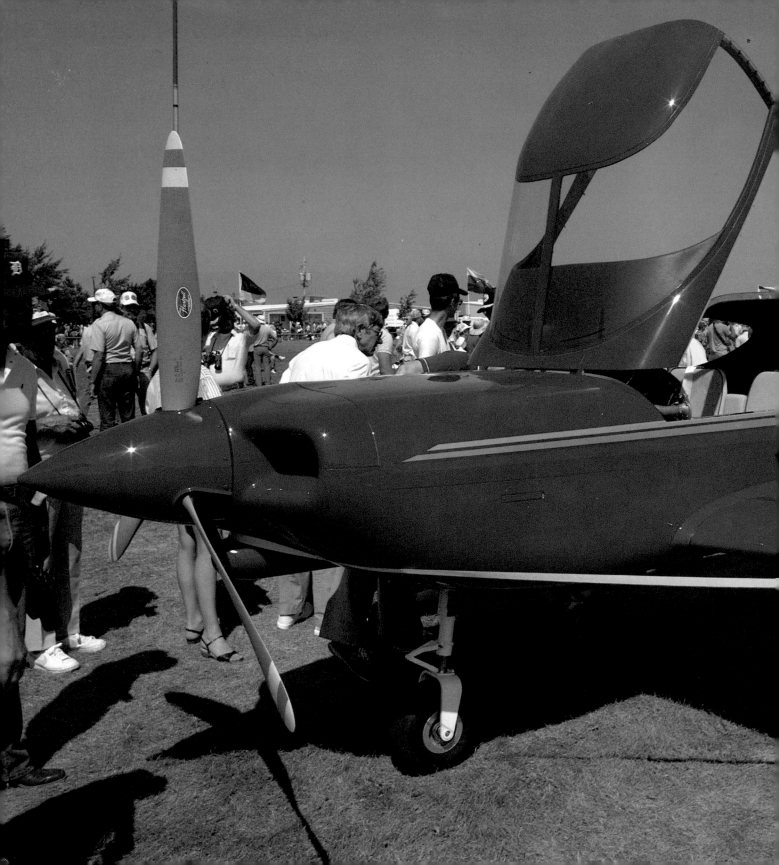

Preceding pages Dick Rutan and Jeana Yeager stole the show in 1984 by bringing Voyager from Mojave. The airplane is designed to fly around the world nonstop and unrefueled on one tankful—nearly 1500 gallons. **These pages** Ed Swearingen's immaculate prototype of the SX-300 metal kitbuilt

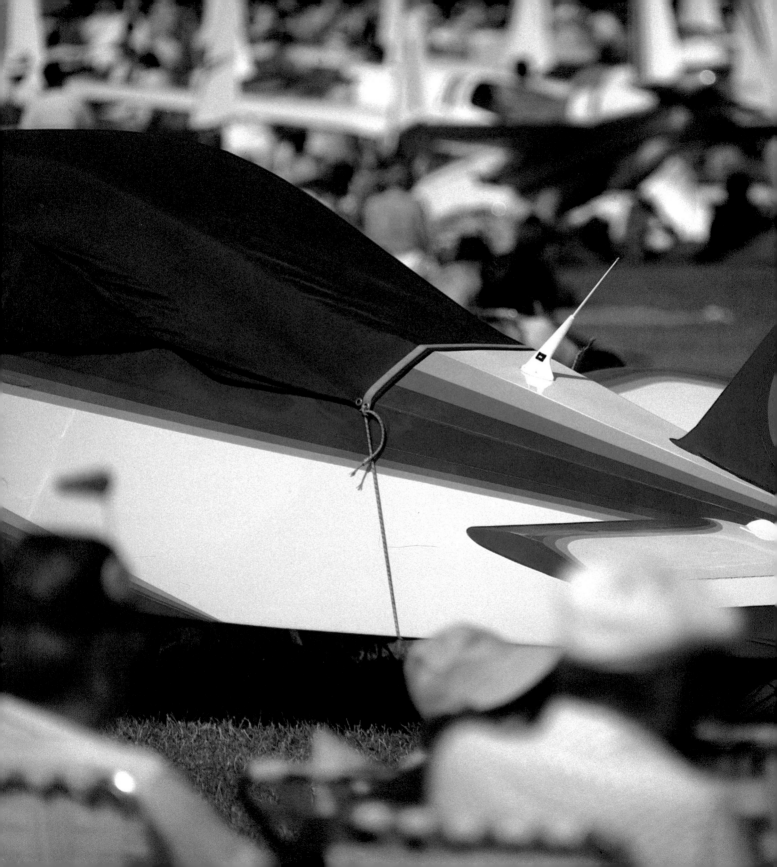

Previous page George Pereira's 200 hp GP 4 was named both Grand Champion Custombuilt and Outstanding New Design. The wood finish was made to look like glass by spraying and rubbing eight gallons of paint. Average groundspeed for the 2225 miles from Sacramento to Oshkosh was 223 mph on 9.4 gallons per hour. **Left** Thorp Super T-18 mingles with the crowd. **Top** 250 hp Barracuda belonging to Meril Lowrey was completed in 1983. **Above** Gary Rudolph's Piel Emeraude

This page The first kitbuilt Falco made its first public appearance at Oshkosh. It belongs to David Aronson of Minneapolis, and was built from a kit developed by Alfred Scott's Sequoia Aircraft, of Richmond, Virginia.
Right Morry Hummel's Hummel Bird weighs a mere 268 lb empty and carries its single occupant at 105 mph

Left A completed BD-5, a relative rarity following manufacturer's difficulties in supplying all the kit parts in the 1970s. **Above** Pober Pixie. The name was derived from the airplane's designer, Paul Poberezny. High wings have other uses, such as sunshades while shooting the breeze

Page 30/31 An earlier Pereira design, the Osprey 2 amphibian. **Preceding pages** Sorrell Hiperbipe **Preceding pages inset left** AeroGare Sea Hawk amphibian, powered by a 150 hp Lycoming O-320. Kits sell for $12,000. **Centre** Stoddard-Hamilton Glasair RG, one of the new breed of high-performance composite kitbuilts. **Right** This Windwagon cost Virgil Hostetler $3600 to build in 1981. It is powered by half a VW engine

Above J. L. Miller's Taylor Titch, a 560 lb single-seater, cost $700 to build in 1972. It is propelled by a Continental C-85 turning a handsome three-blade prop. **Above right** John Monnett's kit-airplane business is a family affair. His wife, Betty, and one of the boys manned the sales booth. **Right** The first Task Research Silhouette kitbuilt, minus some rather important parts, makes its way to the display area, where it was reunited with its wings

EXPERIMENTAL

YOU ARE INVITED
TO LOOK AS
MUCH AS YOU LIKE
BUT *Please* DO NOT
TOUCH!

Homebuilt helicopters are comparatively rare. As the plaque says, this example (the Hummingbird) was not only built by but also designed by its owner, Dick DeGraw. Technically, it was an extremely ambitious project. Power is provided by two 70 hp Volkswagen engines that drive twin, intermeshing, counter-rotating main rotor blades, thereby self-defeating torque and eliminating the need for a tail rotor. DeGraw also designed and built the necessary reduction gearboxes

Above RotorWay Scorpion homebuilt helicopter: putting rotors on dreams, to paraphrase an EAA slogan

This helicopter was designed and built in its entirety by...

Dick DeGraw

EAA CHAPTER 304 Jackson, Mich.

Old Glory: antiques & classics

In spite of its predilection for discarding the old in the name of progress, America has a deep respect for some pieces of its past. Aviation's past, like that of America, is comparatively recent and, thanks to restorers and enthusiasts, it is very much alive in 1985. Some of the immaculate specimens appearing in these pages are probably in better shape than when they were new; all of them reflect in their gleaming finishes an extraordinary amount of care and attention by their owners. Most are faithful to every detail of the original: to sit in and to fly one is to enter a vanished world of polished wood, big instruments and few of them, with

not a glow-winkie or plastic gismo in sight. And the smell—the aroma of old wood and fabric and leather is recaptured to tantalize the nostrils. 'If you wish to smoke, please step outside' . . . 'Real pilots fly taildraggers' . . . 'Real taildraggers fly pilots', read the instrument-panel placards and tee shirts. Baseball caps bear the N number and type of airplane which carried the wearer to this great binge of nostalgia for the days of leather helmets, silk scarves and wind in the wires.

Membership in the EAA's Antique & Classic division is open to all those interested in such airplanes. Its primary aim is to encourage and aid in the

restoration and preservation of antiques and classics. In line with this, it maintains a library on the history of aviation and on specific old aircraft and engines as an aid to their restoration.

An antique is defined as any airplane built by the original manufacturer or licensee before 1946; classics are those that were built between 1946 and 1955 inclusive. Some of the relics that appear at Oshkosh each year have been flying all their lives, but that is by no means always the case. Many have been rescued from ruin by enthusiasts who spotted their wingless or engineless carcases rotting in the long grass of quiet rural airfields. Others are found hanging from the rafters of barns, abandoned and forgotten decades ago. No matter how extensive the delapidation, as long as the manufacturer's plate is still attached, that's all that is required for the restoration to begin. Sometimes a 'restored' antique is actually virtually brand new, the majority of its components having been handbuilt from scratch with reference to the original plans if they exist. Thousands of dollars and hours can go into an extensive rebuild, which explains why the finished article receives so much TLC.

The movement has its roots in the Antique Airplane Association, founded by Robert Taylor of Ottumwa, Iowa. Although the AAA still exists, its annual fly-in, held in Blakesburg, Iowa, does not admit the public, making Oshkosh the place to see these old airplanes in their greatest numbers. Many owners of antiques belong to both the AAA and the EAA's Antiques & Classics division.

Each year at Oshkosh, the restorers' art is recognized by the awarding of trophies for the most outstanding examples. The Classic Grand Champion at Oshkosh 84 was a 1947 Cessna 140, NC4135N, belonging to Rick and Kathie Paige, of San Mateo, California. Its polished aluminum finish could have been used by the convention campers for their morning ablutions. Rick bought the airplane in 1973 and in the ensuing years brought it to Grand Champion condition. Grand Champion Antique was Tom Laurie's 1934 Stinson SR-5E Reliant, which was a basket case when he spotted it in the back of a hangar in 1974. It has been restored to original condition but with modern covering.

Page 40/41 Cessna 195 **Preceding page** 1935 Pasped
Skylark, the only one ever built. Powered by a 165 hp
Warner, the airplane belongs to Bob Greenhoe, of
Alma, Michigan. Empty weight is 1330 lb, gross weight
1930 lb; it cruises at 115 mph. **Above** 1950 Trojan,
with the same cruising speed as the Pasped. The
airplane belongs to Nancy Grout. **Right** 1948
Luscombe 8E with mirror-finish polished aluminum
skin

The standard of workmanship in this restored 1934 Stinson SR-5E won its owner/restorer, Tom Laurie, the Grand Champion Antique Award in 1984. Laurie, a lifelong aeromodeller, is not a licensed pilot, but he spotted the airplane in the back of a hangar at FlaBob Airport, Rubidoux, California, in 1974 and spent a decade rebuilding it from ruin to its current condition

Above 1940 Waco UPF 7, owned by Bill Amundson and Dick Peterson. Power comes from a 220 hp Continental R670

Right de Havilland Canada DHC-1 Chipmunk, for many years the Royal Air Force's primary trainer

Above right Cessna 140 (left) and short-wing Piper provide some shade and shelter for their owners

Many Oshkosh visitors got their first taste of flying in airplanes like these Stearmans, with the bellow of a big radial, its cylinders out in the breeze

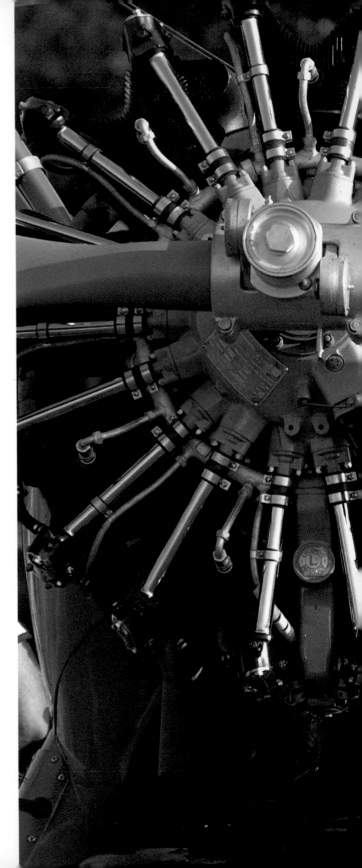

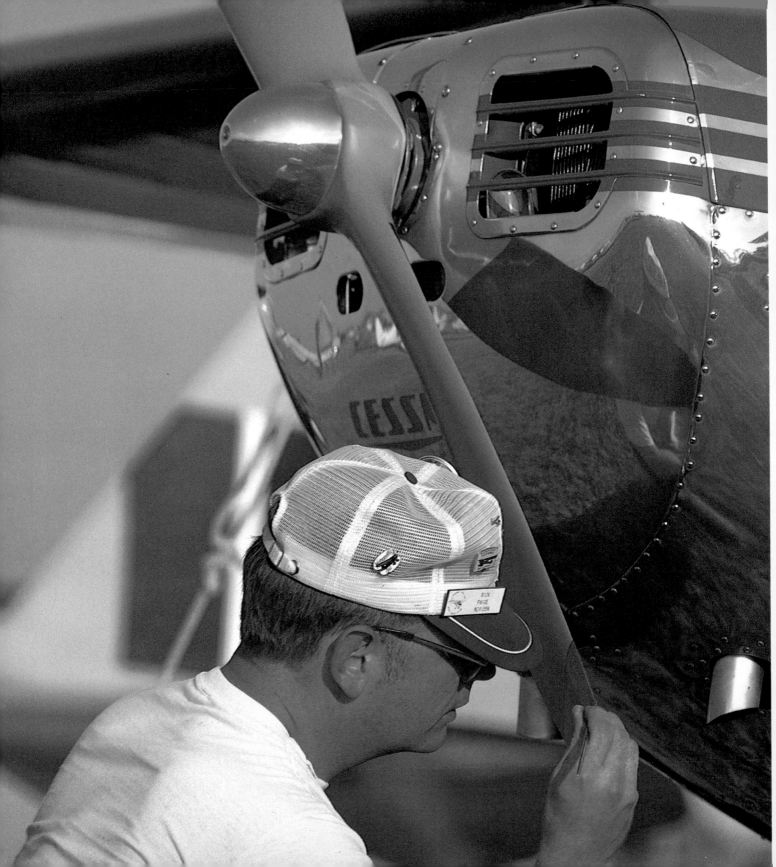

Left· Rick and Kathie Paige's 1947 Cessna 140 was named Grand Champion Classic in 1984. A police officer, Rick affixed a notice in the rear window: 'This Aircraft Protected by Smith & Wesson'

Above Sinister fuselage art applied to a Bücker Jungmann biplane

Preceding page Ryan PT-22, the 'PT' standing for the airplane's role when it was in military service: that of primary trainer

Left In the days of radial engines, fixed gear, interplane struts and flying wires—and cheap fuel— streamlining took a back seat to raw power

Above and overleaf Antiques and classics line-up shows the many configurations of the era

Preceding page Pristine gull-wing Stinson, in the colours of American Airlines route-survey airplane

Above Ken Flaglor's Gee Bee Y, built in 1984 but based on a 1930s design, has a 300 hp Lycoming R-680-13. Hanging from nearly all the display airplanes at Oshkosh is a specifications card giving the leading data. Like many homebuilders, Flaglor left blank the line for 'Cost to build'

Dick Fritz, of Willmar, Minnesota, spent 4000 hours
rebuilding this 1936 Beech C17L Staggerwing, serial
number 103. It was completed in May 1983

MONOCOUPE

Left Production of Monocoupes began in 1927 and continued into the 1950s, long before this admirer was produced

Above This replica of Charles Lindbergh's *Spirit of St. Louis*, the airplane he flew solo from New York to Paris in 1927, was built by the EAA Foundation and flown on a national tour of 107 cities in 48 states to commemorate the fiftieth anniversary of Lindbergh's achievement

NEW
UB
FT CORP.
PA. U.S.A.

ROUTE SUP

Cessna

N9375Æ

FIELD
AFT
ATION
TY, MO.

1929 PIETENPOL
Air Camper

Air show

The world's biggest aviation event would hardly be complete without an air show, so each afternoon heads crank skyward while some of the best known pilots in the business go through their routines. Like the rest of the workforce at Oshkosh, they are unpaid volunteers who do it for love and for the honour of performing before the biggest crowd of aviation people.

In recent years, there has been a growing rivalry between the EAA show and that put on at Harlingen, Texas, by the Confederate Air Force. Warbirds are the centrepiece, and the EAA show is giving the Confederates' Harlingen show a run for its money when it comes to recreating the war part. It's a friendly rivalry—the colonels bring some of their machinery and participate. At Oshkosh 84 the pyrotechnic displays

reached a new high, as dozens of gas barrels exploded beneath the CAF's Boeing B-29 Superfortress, *FiFi*, as it overflew the runway. Although the barrels were being exploded a few hundred yards from the crowd line, the earth shook and the heat could be felt at the instant they erupted in broiling clouds of reddish gold. Whether or not you agree with the glorification of aerial bombardment, the show is undeniably spectacular, the logical extension to the display of preserved warbirds.

Oshkosh has become famous for many of its facets, among them the mass flypasts by AT-6/SNJ-5/Harvard World War II trainers. The most widely operated of warbirds, these old growlers formate en masse and rumble overhead, 30 at a time, bringing back vivid

memories to those who once heard the sound as a battle cry.

And then there are the aerobatic routines—Bob Lyjak in his Waco Taperwing, Bob Herendeen and his Pitts Special, Duane Cole and his deadstick routine in a clipped-wing Taylorcraft, Earl and Paula Cherry in the big Stearman, *General Smoke*, so named for the density of its display smoke. One airplane, however, carrying a man and a woman, stole the show in 1984. Burt Rutan's Voyager, with only 10 flights logged, came to Oshkosh from its Mojave home base and awed the crowd with its size, frailty and grace. Aboard the airplane were the two people who were intending to fly Voyager nonstop and unrefueled around the world, Dick Rutan (Burt's brother) and Jeana Yeager. Voyager's fuel capacity is 1489 gallons, 40 percent of which would be enough for the airplane to break the then current unrefuelled distance record, set in 1962 by a B-52H that flew 12,532 miles.

Voyager appeared overhead Oshkosh six hours before there was a landing slot, so Rutan and Yeager orbited the field at 11,500 ft for a whole afternoon before beginning the slow descent onto Wittman Field. With the air show finished, Voyager's eerie shape grew larger with each descending turn, until the airplane was at pattern altitude. Burt Rutan's radio communications with brother Dick at Voyager's controls were fed into the public-address system, for all to hear. When asked if Jeana would like to say a few words, Dick replied that the landing-gear motor was busy at present. Although they would share the flying on the round-the-world attempt, one of Jeana's jobs was to wind down each landing gear by hand, using a lightweight winch around which she wrapped and wound each retraction/extension cable, one at a time. This novel actuation system was one of many weight-saving measures aimed at maximizing Voyager's range and fuel capacity. If the airplane performed as predicted, it would have a range of 25,000 miles on one tankful.

To watch Rutan and Yeager circle Wittman Field and touch down delicately at 40 knots was to watch something destined for the record book and a place in history. How often do you see 100,000 people awed into silence?

Preceding pages, left Earl and Paula Cherry and Stearman *General Smoke* in full flatulence. **Right** Bob and Pat Wagner take a bow after landing. **This page, right** Jim Mynning flies while Eddie Green climbs aboard from a speeding Buick

70

Above Bob Griffin shows the spectacular STOL capabilities of the first production Helio Courier

Right Dr Bob Lyjak is renowned for his spirited display in a Waco Taperwing

Jim Mynning again, this time landing his Piper Cub on 'the world's smallest aircraft carrier.' **Right** Earl Cherry and *General Smoke* laying another trail. The smoke is produced by injecting oil into the exhaust pipe, where it ignites. Nobody does it more billowing than Cherry and his Stearman

Warbirds

'The difference between the men and the boys,' the saying goes, 'is the price of their toys. And he who dies with the most toys wins.' At Oshkosh, the warbirds are as expensive as they come. And, like a certain charge card, a warbird says more about you than any mere airplane ever can. The idea of owning what was once ordered by an air force and perhaps flown in combat holds a particular fascination for some private individuals who are wealthy enough to foot the bills.

Some flew their airplane type as young men in uniform, and for them there must be a strong element of satisfaction with being successful enough in later life to actually buy one of the most exciting parts of their

past. Imagine the kick, 30 years from now, of flying your own F-16.

Apart from being historically significant, most warbirds are obscenely powerful, far in excess of anything with propellers that can be bought new today. This would seem to be one of the strong draws of these old battle axes, because a lot of warbird enthusiasts were born long after the airplanes had been retired from active duty. A warbird's pistons have a power that goes beyond the mere propulsion of an airframe; they can also evoke nostalgia in someone who was never there. They represent an era when you could see, simply by looking, how a machine worked—the throw

of a locomotive's steam piston to the connecting rod to the wheels to the track, the thunderous clatter of an airplane's pistons turning propeller blades churning chunks of air as it dragged itself aloft.

The rallying cry of the EAA's Warbirds of America division, 'Keep 'em Flying,' aptly sums up its aims. Although preserving a warbird in non-flying condition is preferable to turning it into beer cans or automobile trim, something is missing—the way a stuffed animal in a zoo would be wrong. Returning a derelict World War II airplane to flying trim can be a monumental task of restoration, replacement, and searching for components. The days when airplanes were discarded by the thousands as the garbage of war have gone, and finding abandoned military airplanes now involves delving deeply into military records and searching worldwide. A search got under way in 1983 for six Lockheed P-38 Lightnings and two Boeing B-17 Flying Fortresses that are known to have been abandoned on the frozen wastes of Greenland in World War II, following a massed forced landing during an Atlantic crossing. The airplanes are buried in between 40 and 60 ft of snow, but the recovery team believes they are essentially intact. In 1983 the airplanes were located, but they had yet to be exhumed by the end of 1984.

Only single specimens remain of some warbirds, and against the pleasure provided by their return to flying, the risks have to be weighed. Although the unique specimens are flown and maintained with meticulous care, accidents do happen. In most cases, the benefits are deemed to outweigh the risks, and the airplanes fly.

As with the EAA's other divisions, membership in the Warbirds of America is open not only to owners but to anyone interested.

Left Lockheed P-38 Lightning

Overleaf Douglas A-26, with machine guns that could be heard firing blanks in flight

Above Beech T-34 Mentors are popular for their handling characteristics and because they are relatively inexpensive 'warbirds' of a sort. **Right** Mass AT-6/SNJ flypast, accompanied by the deep music of dozens of radials

Left Flying formation with one airplane demands concentration; flying with dozens of others calls for supreme discipline as well. The mass flypasts are one aspect of the show that people talk about whenever the subject of the Oshkosh air show arises. The sight and sound is unusual enough these days that it becomes etched deeply into memories

Overleaf An SNJ-5 tucks up its feet after a typically deafening take-off. The propeller's diameter and its speed of rotation combine to put tip speed in the transonic range with full power and fine pitch, giving the powerplant its distinctive rasp

AT-6s/SNJ-5s are popular now for the same reasons they were liked in the military. They were and still are trainers. Today they prepare pilots for more potent warbirds, such as P-51 Mustangs, just as they did in the 1940s. 'Tee-Six Time' is a prerequisite of being let loose in the rarer machinery, although many a P-51 pilot says the old trainer is more demanding to fly than the fancy ones. Not all AT-6 owners, however, have their eye on the more exotic warbirds; most are happy to fly the T-6 for its own sake, rather than for what it could be preparing them to fly. It is a demanding airplane, and thus a satisfying one

Overleaf A pair of T-34s take off to formate for another mass flypast

Preceding page Despite its barrel-chested look, the T-28 is one of the nicest flying warbirds. It replaced the AT-6 as the Air Force's mainstay trainer. **Above** Junkers Ju-52, Teutonic Tin Goose. **Below** Immaculate T-34 Mentor. **Right** Hawker Sea Fury owned by an airline pilot who made 50 trips to England for parts and advice during its restoration

Upward mobility for the masses

Hang gliders were fun, but their uses were somewhat limited. First you needed a slope or a cliff, and then you needed the wind to blow if you were to stay aloft for any time. It was inevitable that sooner or later somebody would strap on an engine. When hang gliders evolved from the sailwing Rogallo 'kite' type and grew rigid wings, the transition to power was just around the corner. Chainsaw and snowmobile engines were tried first; they produced about 20 hp and sipped fuel at the rate of just a gallon an hour. Empty weights were around 150 pounds, and people began to wonder just what these contraptions were. If they were airplanes, they would need regulating; but if they were literally powered hang gliders, was certification necessary or fair?

As the ultralights became heavier, faster and potentially capable of more damage, the question became more vexing. Why should these unregulated machines and unlicensed pilots be allowed access to the airspace when pilots of conventional airplanes had had to study and practice for the privilege? Why should existing pilots have to share the skies with people who were not required to know even the basic rules of the

Left Chuck Yeager's American Aircraft Falcon

Below Zenair Zipper and (**overleaf**) Lazair, both with one engine per seat

air? Why, in the name of personal freedom, shouldn't they, replied the ultralight proponents.

Not long ago, some requirements were agreed upon. To be classified as an ultralight and to be made exempt from airplane and pilot certification requirements, an ultralight can weigh no more than 254 lb empty, carry no more than one seat and five gallons of fuel, cruise no faster than 55 mph and stall no faster than 26 mph. The weight limit was high enough for designers not to compromise structural integrity, and it signalled the beginning of the ultralight's maturity.

Despite the design requirements, ultralight pilots remain unlicensed at the time of writing, and there are rumblings that regulation is inevitable. Thanks to a few widely publicised and gruesome accidents, and many minor mishaps, ultralights still have a poor safety image. But they have also made the headlines in a more positive light, by flying from coast to coast and on charitable fund-raising flights, for example. Ultralights have brought flight to people who otherwise would not have flown, and to a very limited extent there has been some crossover of ultralight pilots to full-size aviation— although not as great as some had hoped.

If you parallel the growth of ultralights and full-size aviation, ranking the first micros with the Wright Flyer, then ultralights are probably at the Piper Cub stage today. They have acquired enclosed cockpits, solid airfoil section wings, rather than sailcloth stretched over tubes, and some are adopting modern materials technology such as graphite.

The EAA Ultralight Association encourages high standards from its members through the Ultralight Flight Log Achievement Program. Ultralights are a part of the annual EAA convention, with their own display and flying area, but they also have their own convention, again at Oshkosh, a month or so before the main event. A well spent hour is to wander down to the ultralight operating area as evening falls: the wind drops, and the frail-looking ragwings buzz aloft, their skin catching the colours of a midwestern sunset as they follow each other around the flyby pattern, maybe 30 at a time. They have been given unflattering labels by the cynics—'flying lawn furniture' . . . 'self-launching gibbets'—but there is no denying the appeal of the ultralights as they float slowly over pastures of grazing cattle, capturing flight in its simplest form.

Above and overleaf Teratorn Tierra, with a 1984 kit
price at $4295. **Above right** Inspired by the Fokker
Eindecker, this ultralight has an empty weight of 240 lb
and is powered by a 27 hp Rotax. It is a product of
The Airplane Factory, Dayton, Ohio. **Right** Eipper,
one of the larger ultralight manufacturers, sells its
Quicksilver with the pizzazz of big business. This one
is a 'GT' model with some drag-reducing refinements

Preceding pages This Buccaneer ultralight, like the original full-size airplane Lake Buccaneer, is amphibious, allowing it to walk, swim, and fly. **Above** How do you find the weight of an ultralight? You put it on the scales, of course, and shield it from the lifting effect of the wind by doing it in a hangar. **Right** Maxair Drifter drifting in. **Overleaf** Although the Breezy came along before the ultralights (and does not classify as one because of weight, speed, and seating capacity), the spirit of open-air thrills is just the same. **Page 110/111** Pinaire Ultra-Aire

The essence of Oshkosh

How could you explain the coming together of well over half a million people and virtually no litter, no booze, no crime, no rowdiness, no badness at all? Oshkosh is hallowed ground, The Great Congregation of Flying. Many a family spends its entire annual vacation allotment on the pilgrimage to the shrine. The crowds have a respect for the event that shows they regard their presence more as a participation than a visit. With occasional chivying over the PA loudspeakers, the attendees leave behind them almost no sign of their passing. When the event is over, the grass is flattened except for the outlines where wings and fuselages shielded the turf from the herd. Otherwise there are none of the usual signs of a human massing—no cigarette butts, candy wrappers or soda cans. The site is left the way it was found. And despite their fragility, nearly all the airplanes escape the curiosity of the crowd with barely a fingerprint.

During the convention, Oshkosh is the world's busiest airport, handling four times more take-offs and landings than Chicago O'Hare. Visitors come from every state and from 100 foreign countries, filling motel rooms, campgrounds and college dorms for a radius of 60 miles. Forty thousand people camp on the site itself. In effect, a small town springs up for a week, complete with shops, public phones, showers and evening theatre featuring musicians, entertainers and classic aviation films. Accommodations on site range from simple tents to motorhomes costing as much as high-performance airplanes, cosseting their residents with everything from air conditioning to microwave cooking.

The days are spent browsing through the rows of airplanes on static display, inspecting the old and the new, chatting with fellow builders and pilots and exchanging ideas and tips. In the Fly Market, EAA's version of a flea market, there are plenty of ways to slim your wallet. Most of the wares are aviation related, ranging from toy airplanes and airplane sculptures to tee shirts, used engines and instruments and books.

Although the EAA is the voice of the 'little man' in aviation, the big aircraft manufacturers can't pass up the opportunity to display their products before such an enormous audience. Cessna, Beech, Piper and Mooney bring a variety of aircraft, ranging from pressurized singles to light twins. The majority of fly-in visitors to Oshkosh come in factory-built airplanes spanning the whole range—two-seat singles to jets—and potential customers are plentiful.

In the exhibit halls, there are customers aplenty for the homebuilding suppliers, who peddle everything from landing-gear legs and cowlings to upholstery and plans. The exhibit booths offer the chance for builders to meet with designers.

Preceding pages Oshkosh B'Gosh overalls, the town's other claim to fame. And airplanes as far as the eye can see, by gosh. **Below** Jay Frey, who runs EDO's floats division, gets some help moving his amphibious Cessna Turbo Stationair 6

The regular and extra controllers who man the
Oshkosh tower are the busiest in the world during the
annual convention. ATC at Oshkosh is, for the pilots,
primarily a matter of keeping quiet. There is simply
too much traffic for each pilot to have much of a say
over the radio, beyond initially announcing his arrival
in the vicinity. This is the speediest ATC a pilot is
ever likely to encounter: clipped, rapid-fire orders to
the 'blue and white Cherokee you're number seven
following a Stearman rock your wings red and white
Bellanca keep your speed up you've got a Twin
Comanche right behind you and Baron on final caution

wake turbulence from departing Dash 7 red Aerostar you're supposed to be following that 210 just off to your right that's good er Baron land long you've got a P-51 behind you okay Cessna 38 Juliet just a little longer. . .' and so on and on, until some 14,000 airplanes have alighted at Oshkosh

Overleaf Ardy & Ed's drive-in, on the shore of Lake Winnebago and beneath the final approach to Oshkosh, is a popular off-airport eating spot. The food isn't bad, but, more important, you can watch airplanes while tucking into a Steak-Um Basket and chocolate shake

Left With volunteers placed all over the convention site's sprawl to direct and park airplanes, man gates and booths, thirst was a problem under the August sun. Hence 'Operation Thirst,' which dispensed soda and lemonade and sandwiches to oil the many cogs of Oshkosh

Above It's back again, for the umpteenth time since 1929; the Great Lakes Biplane is now in production in Claremont, New Hampshire

Left Ed Swearingen was much in demand by homebuilders with questions about his new kitbuilt, the SX-300, which was shown publicly for the first time at Oshkosh 84 shortly after its first flight. **Right** Chuck Yeager, he of Mach 1 fame, was asked by an interviewer from a local TV station whether he had seen the movie, *The Right Stuff*. To which Yeager replied quietly, 'Er, yes. I acted in it'

Below Just like it says on the label